Journeys
of Joy

Journeys
of Joy

30
TRUE STORIES
of Abundant Living

Collected by Allison Gappa Bottke
Founder of the God Allows U-Turns Project,
with Cheryll Hutchings

BARBOUR
PUBLISHING

The author is represented by Alive Communications, Inc., 7680 Goddard St., Suite 200, Colorado Springs, Colorado 80920.

Published by Barbour Publishing, Inc., P.O. Box 719, Uhrichsville, Ohio 44683
www.barbourbooks.com

Our mission is to publish and distribute inspirational products offering exceptional value and biblical encouragement to the masses.

Member of the
Evangelical Christian
Publishers Association

Printed in the United States of America.
5 4 3 2 1

Contents

Introduction

If you were to define joy, how would you do it?

Scripture gives us clues. For starters, Nehemiah 8:10 tells us the joy of the Lord is our strength. First Chronicles 16:27 tells us that strength and joy are in God's dwelling place. John 16:24 tells us to ask and we'll receive so that our joy will be full. John 16:20 promises that our grief will turn to joy.

No matter what definition of joy we use—abundance, happiness, fulfillment, whatever—our relationship with God is integral to true joy in our lives.

The thirty stories in this book outline the authors' journeys to joy and abundant living. Through these true stories, the authors show us different perspectives of what it means to rejoice in the Lord. Our prayer is that as you read them, you'll be challenged and inspired. You might relate very closely to some of these stories. Others will give you hope and help as you seek to overcome the difficulties in your life. Some might teach you a bit about finding your joy in Christ. And some of these testimonials will lead you to simply smile or celebrate the goodness of the Lord.

May the joy of the Lord become the center of your life!

Midnight Serenade
by Sandra J. Campbell, Garden City, Michigan

I slowly descended the stairs, hurting more with each step. "Mike, I think I need to go to the hospital," I whimpered. I had been sick for three weeks and had already been through two rounds of antibiotics. My fever was back up to 104 degrees. The light hurt my eyes. Every part of me ached. I tried to rest but awoke feeling worse than before. "Something must be wrong. I'm just not getting any better," I lamented.

Mike agreed and took me to the emergency room at St. Mary's Hospital, where the doctors poked and prodded, trying to figure out the problem. After five hours of blood tests and X-rays, they decided to admit me.

Meanwhile, the pain came in waves. First my head pounded, then my eyes blurred, then the fever spiked, and awful pain traveled throughout my body. The doctor had no clue as to what was wrong.

"Must be a virus," he said.

Late that night a woman was admitted to my semiprivate

room. She was obviously feeling great pain, and I learned she had come up from surgery. She woke me from a fitful sleep as she yelled hysterically at the nurses.

"Give me pain medication. My doctor said I wouldn't have any pain. Give me something now!" she screamed.

Guess I'm not getting any sleep tonight, I thought, as my head started pounding again.

The nurses refused her demands, and I heard her make a phone call to her husband. "Come and get me right now! I want outta here! I have medicine at home if they won't give it to me here. If you won't come and get me, I'll call a cab!" she wailed.

She slammed the phone and yelled some more. This was going to be a long night.

I shuffled into the bathroom, pulling my IV pole with me. *Lord, how can I help this woman?* I prayed. On the way back to my bed, I stuck my head behind her curtain and said, "I'm sorry you are in so much pain. Is there anything I can do to help?"

She immediately calmed down and said her doctor had promised her she would not have any pain, but the nurses would not listen to her plea for medicine. I told her I was a Christian and asked if I could have a word of prayer with her. I motioned to the crucifix on the wall and gently reminded her that Jesus knew all about pain and suffering.

I held her hand and prayed, "Lord, we thank You that You are the Great Physician. Thank You that You care about our suffering. Thank You that You were willing to suffer for us by dying on the cross in our place. You know just what we are going through right now. I ask You to please comfort this dear lady, ease her pain, and help us praise Your name even now in this place. In Jesus' name, amen."

She thanked me and told me that she, too, was a believer. The Holy Spirit gave me the courage to ask her if she had heard of a song called "Promises." I asked if I could sing it for her. "Please do," she said.

Normally, I am shy. When I sing with the ladies' trio at church, I stand in the middle so they can hold me up if I start to crumple! I would never dream of offering a solo. But here I was, at midnight, singing a cappella in a darkened hospital room! I don't remember who wrote the song, but I softly sang it to her.

My voice trembled and cracked out the song I learned so long ago. Somewhere between my feeble attempt and my roommate's ears, God changed that song into a beautiful melody that encouraged her heart. She asked, "Could you please sing it again? That was just beautiful!" she exclaimed. I timidly complied.

Then I had an idea. "Do you know any praise choruses?" I asked.

"A few," she replied.

"Why don't we sing them together?" I suggested.

There we were. Strangers, yet sisters in the Lord. We softly sang together sweet songs of faith, and we were blessed. I remembered the story in Acts 16:25–26 about when Paul and Silas sang and prayed in prison at midnight. Their chains fell off, and God delivered them from prison. Then I thought about how when we sing and praise God for His goodness, our chains of pain and discouragement break and our spirits are free to worship our Lord.

After an hour or so, I bade her good night, and we slept soundly the rest of the night. I heard her talking on the phone the next morning with friends and noticed that her whole attitude had changed. Later that day her husband came to take her home. She was in such a sweet frame of mind that he asked what had come over her. She told him, "The Lord sent an angel to pray and sing with me last night."

Now that's the first time anyone other than my husband has called me an angel! I do know as I yielded myself to the Lord that He answered my prayer for help. He gave me clear direction and the boldness I needed to be a blessing to a stranger. Together we sang psalms, hymns, and spiritual songs, making melody in our hearts to the Lord.

A Lesson in Forgiveness
by Joan Clayton, Portales, New Mexico

Annie's day started out all wrong. The other children complained about the insults and mistreatment she was inflicting. I took Annie aside and whispered quietly. She vehemently denied doing anything wrong. When Eddie reported that Annie had pinched him (the redness of his arm corroborated the story), I asked Annie to stay in the room with me during recess.

At recess time, Annie sat down and finished her math. Eddie stayed in to finish his math, too. They both brought their papers to me about the same time. I checked them and said to her, "Do you have something to say to Eddie?"

She looked at Eddie. "I'm so sorry. I don't know why I did that. I really wish I wouldn't do things like that."

"That's okay." Eddie's chin quivered, but he completely forgave.

The other children came in from recess, and we settled down for story time. I noticed that Annie didn't join us.

Since she had offended so many other children, she was holding back, but deep down, I felt she wanted to be part of the group.

I pulled her close and said, "Do you have something you want to say to the other children?" I breathed a sigh of relief as she walked to the front of the class. But when she stood in front of the group, she became hostile again. I asked Annie to return to her seat and told her that when she had something to say, she could rejoin the group. I prayed all the while that I was doing the right thing.

As I read the last page of the story to the children, Annie came to me and whispered, "I have something to say." She began, "I'm sorry I've been mean to all of you. I'm sorry I pulled your hair. I didn't mean to kick you. I'm sorry I spat on you. I really don't want to be that way!"

Spontaneously, the children cheered. Annie smiled as she sat down among the group. Even though the children had not mistreated her, they began to say, "We're sorry, too! We didn't treat you right either." It happened just that simply—over and done with. Case closed. Yes, other infractions of the rules might occur, but they must be dealt with as they happened. This incident ended.

When do we lose that ability to forgive? Where, in that transition from childhood to adulthood, do we hang on to not forgiving? We visualize instant replays of some incident that happened months, even years ago. Every time it is replayed, we again feel the unjust wounds and the anger that festers in the unhealed places in our minds.

I made a U-turn that day. I resolved to choose to have the forgiving, loving spirit of a child. I learned to look within myself. Even though I thought the other children had not offended Annie, they, too, searched within, seeking to make things right.

I'm so thankful for children. They continue to teach me, just as scripture does when it refers to their innocent wisdom: "Of such is the kingdom of heaven" (Matthew 19:14 NKJV).

Sometimes There Are No U-Turns
by Shanna Hoskison, Pecan Gap, Texas

Early in 1982, we weren't exactly planning to have a child. Ideally, we had wanted to wait five years before starting a family. Two years into our marriage, those plans changed. Our daughter was conceived.

At twenty years of age, I didn't think too much about it. I was too young to be worried, scared, or expectant in any way. Being pregnant and having babies was what everyone was doing. We were no different.

Our baby was perfect in every way, with a wonderful disposition. Except for some typical thirteen-year-old rebellion, she grew to be a wonderful child. She was a good student, loved by peers and teachers, and she always made us proud. As she grew up, though, I wanted a sibling for her. Coming from a family of five children, I couldn't imagine not having a brother or a sister. I wanted this for my daughter. She deserved the closeness of a sibling. But it just didn't seem to be God's plan. As she turned eight, nine, ten, I resolved myself to raising an only child.

When she turned sixteen, I began to prepare myself for the "empty nest" syndrome. I had no idea how God would help me through this. Then I began to feel what I had only felt one other time in my life, some seventeen years before. I ignored the symptoms for some time, thinking my mind must be playing tricks on me. My body had to be going through some phase.

Surely I wasn't pregnant.

Oh, but I was.

I wasn't sure how I would explain this to my firstborn, but this was a path that had no U-turns. I remember crying for two days and nights, my husband consoling me. When I called my mother to ask her for wisdom, she said, "God doesn't make mistakes." When I told my seventeen-year-old that I was expecting, she simply looked to heaven and said, "Well, it's got to be God, after all these years. You may be carrying a prophet, great leader, or who knows, but I know this baby has a very special calling on its life."

We now have a young daughter of only a few months. Our daughters are seventeen years apart in age. Was this our plan? No. This was definitely God's plan for our lives. It surely wasn't ours.

As I watch her in her walker, running across the kitchen floor chasing the stream of light from the window,

I laugh. My oldest says I think everything the baby does is funny. I explain, no, it's just when I think about how I felt when I found out about her that I have to laugh. I have to laugh at the tears I shed and the hesitancy and fear I felt when I first found out I was pregnant. Accompanying my laughter is an abiding thankfulness for God's wisdom and His plan for my life.

I am so glad that He is driving this car called "Life" instead of me. I never would have taken this road myself. And I would have missed so much.

God's Plan—Not Mine
by Joel Holtz, Minneapolis, Minnesota

I had it all figured out. I was finally moving back to live in
one of my favorite places, central Oregon. My job was ending,
my condo had a buyer, I had gotten rid of all my furniture, and
I was set to leave in a couple of weeks. It had been over ten
years since I had last lived in Oregon, and I could hardly wait
to get back. The Deschutes River, the mountains and forests,
and the aqua blue lakes constantly filled my mind. What
would I do first? Maybe some white-water rafting or a hike in
the forest. Maybe a drive along the Cascade Lakes Highway. I
was following my own path, charting my own course, never
expecting the Lord might have other plans.

After leaving church one Sunday morning, I noticed
someone had left a note on my car windshield. Just weeks
before, I had put a notice in the church bulletin asking for
help with after-church refreshments. Since I was leaving, I
thought I should try and find a replacement to pour water
and coffee, which had been my job for the last couple of

years. I figured the note was about that request.

As I started to read the note, however, it became evident that the person who wrote it was not responding to the notice for help with refreshments but was wondering if I was married.

"Someone in church who knows my car is playing a practical joke," I thought. But then why would she leave a name and a phone number? When I got home, I decided to call the number. I got an answering machine, left my name and number, and, having gotten rid of my bed a few days earlier, promptly took an afternoon nap on my carpeted living room floor.

Later that night the phone rang. It was the person who had left the note.

"This must be Joel. Hi, I'm Rita," she said.

After talking for a few minutes, I felt I had to be totally honest with her.

"I would love to get together with you sometime, but I'm moving to Oregon in a couple of weeks."

"Oh sure, I finally get the nerve to meet someone new, and now you are leaving," she responded with a lilt in her voice.

"Well, I would be happy to take you out to dinner before I go," I offered, not knowing why I had even suggested it.

"I would like that," she said. "My birthday is next week; how about then?"

"Sure, that would be great," I said, again wondering what I was doing.

"Don't you want to know what I look like?" she asked.

"That would make me rather shallow, wouldn't it?" I responded. We were off to a flying start.

We both had a busy week ahead, so we decided to meet the following Friday for dinner. She gave me directions to her home, and I found myself looking forward to the day. I was pleasantly surprised to find her home in one of my favorite areas. When she answered the door, standing before me was one of the most beautiful women I had ever seen.

"I know you," I said, relieved that in fact she was someone I had seen in church before.

We had a great time at dinner that night, and when I drove her home, she invited me inside to continue our conversation. We talked until 2:00 in the morning, at which time I realized I probably would not be moving back to Oregon. As I left to go home, I asked if I could see her again.

"Of course," she answered, smiling.

As so often happens, God had a plan that did not coincide with mine. Thankfully, I followed His lead and not my own.

We have been married now for almost three years. I never made it back to Oregon, and you know what? It doesn't bother me a bit.

Mabel's Miracle
by Charles S. McKinstry, Roanoke, Virginia

Mabel was sixty-seven years old and had been a "goer" and a "doer" all of her life. As a leader in her church, she never missed any opportunity to serve. She was indefatigable, dedicated to praising God by leading an exemplary life.

In December of 1998, Mabel suffered her first heart attack while caring for children whose mothers were at work. She was rushed to the nearest hospital emergency room gasping from chest pains. After she endured a needle in the heart and an EKG, she was hooked up to a beeping monitor, a respirator, and a feeding tube.

Five days later she had recovered enough to function without the tubes and needles and was allowed to sit in the easy chair in her hospital room. Two days of slow walks around the halls produced no further signs of a heart malfunction, so Mabel was sent home to rest and fully regain her strength. Unfortunately, rest was not a word in Mabel's vocabulary. She jumped right in, doing whatever needed to be done. The following week she collapsed again in the church kitchen. Clutching her chest with both hands, she petitioned God, "Take me home now, Father, if I can no longer serve You."

This time she lapsed into unconsciousness as the medics worked on her lifeless body during the siren-screaming ride to the hospital. They were in touch with the emergency room personnel by radio, so everything was ready when they wheeled her through the swinging doors. A heart specialist worked on her faltering heart for two hours before declaring her condition critical but stable. They had no sooner made this pronouncement than the alarms went off and the monitor showed a straight line, indicating that Mabel's heart had stopped.

The respirator, IV, and other lifesaving paraphernalia were put into action again. Mabel later told us she observed all the activity from a vantage point overhead. But she could hear a voice telling her that she must return to tackle the job that God had lined up for her. When technicians administered the electric shock paddles to her chest, she watched her body jerk on the gurney. Finally, the monitor showed a heartbeat again.

Mabel survived and was ultimately transferred to a critical care unit for a week, and then to a private room. Three weeks after she had been revived from death, Mabel was strong enough for a series of extensive tests that would determine the amount of damage.

The results were not encouraging. She had four blocked arteries, limiting the blood that flowed through her heart. She needed quadruple bypass surgery immediately. However, the operating room and the surgeons were fully scheduled until six weeks away. The doctors convinced Mabel to go home and rest, to build up her strength so she could hope to survive the long and dangerous operation.

Mabel rested for the first two days at home. She was too weak to do much else. Her daughter came and took care of her. The third day, though, she bounced out of bed at the first light of morning, said a prayer, got dressed, drank some coffee, and headed for the front door.

"Mama, you get back to bed," her daughter admonished.

"No, dear, the Lord needs me, and I'm going to do His work," she said. With that, she kept busy until the day of her bypass operation.

She walked into the hospital looking like the picture of health, rather than a woman close to death from a blood-starved heart. The doctors couldn't believe she looked and sounded so vibrant, but they had no idea that Mabel knew God wanted her for a job He needed done.

In surgery, when they opened her chest, moved aside

the ribs, and examined her heart and arteries, they were amazed. The four blocked arteries were pale and unhealthy, as they had suspected, but Mabel's heart was pumping blood like a sixteen-year-old's heart.

"That's impossible," the doctor said, shaking his head. "Her heart should be struggling to pump, not acting like a teenager's." Then the surgeon saw something that had not appeared on the latest MRI. A new artery, beautifully pink and pulsing with life, was feeding blood to Mabel's heart. It had apparently developed since her first MRI and accounted for her remarkable preoperative performance.

After Mabel returned to her room, the doctor visited her. "I've been opening chests and examining hearts and arteries for twenty years," he said. "This is the first homemade bypass I've ever seen. It's truly a miracle. I doubted that you would be alive for this operation; now I can see why you are."

Mabel smiled broadly and said, "I hope those three man-made bypasses are as good as the one God gave me, 'cause I'm going to need all the energy I can get. My daughter just lost her husband, and she has to go back to work. I'm going to be a full-time nanny to my two-year-old twin grandsons, and that takes a lot of get-up-and-go!" Then she exclaimed with glee, "Doctor, God has work He wants me to do before He takes me home."

The Extraordinary Faith of a Dung Catcher
as told to Sharon Doorasamy, Westville, South Africa

When I was a boy growing up in South Africa, I prided myself on being the best dung catcher on the sugarcane estate where my father was a laborer. To achieve this high position required two important attributes: an ability to run fast and an understanding of the nature of cows.

We needed the cow dung to keep down the dust in our dirt-floored cinder block house. We would mix the dung with water and splatter it onto the ground to seal the dirt. So, at least once a week, I ventured into the fields to collect fresh dung left to cool on the ground with flies on it. However, to get fresh dung, you must pay attention to when a cow lifts its tail. So when I spotted a tail raising, I'd dash to the cow with my bucket and try to catch the dung before it hit the ground.

I never cared that we were poor until I started high school. Then I realized that the teachers favored the students from "good" homes. I began to compare myself to other children who wore nice clothes, ate bologna sand-wiches, and brought their lunches in neat bags with plastic ties. I ate leftovers from dinner—usually beans or potatoes smashed between two slices of bread. My mother wrapped my sandwiches in newspaper.

Every evening at our home, my mother gathered us together for family worship. She couldn't read well, so one of us children read the scripture she chose. The scripture one night was from Jeremiah 29:11, where the Lord says, "For I know the plans I have for you. . .plans to prosper you and not to harm you, plans to give you hope and a future." I took that passage to heart and was a different person after that night. I never again compared myself to anyone. With the Lord's promise as a comfort and shield, I excelled in my schoolwork and my Christian walk.

I graduated from high school but had no money to go to university. Since these were the days of apartheid, it seemed I had no reason to hope. Yet I was full of hope anyway. I believed God's promise to prosper me and give me a future. And He did, by way of an American mis-sionary who paid my first semester tuition. After that, I won scholarships and awards, which covered the cost of tuition for seven years of full-time study. I was even awarded a Fulbright scholarship to study environmental law at the American University in Washington, D.C.

Today my life is far different from my poor beginnings. I'm an environmental lawyer. Through God's grace I am what I am. How else does one explain how a boy whose parents could not afford to buy him a fifty-cent ball has achieved what I have?

The best dung catcher ever, I am living testimony to the truth that "in all things God works for the good of those who love him" (Romans 8:28).

The Soup Ladle

by Claudia C. Breland, Maple Valley, Washington

Sometimes when I'm standing at the kitchen sink doing dishes, I'll glance up at the curtain rod where I've hung a stainless steel soup ladle. It looks odd up there, hanging down from its curved handle, but I've put it there because it's part of our family history. It also reminds us that we can survive the difficulties of life.

My husband, Richard, often tells the story of what occurred when he was only two years old. After being away all weekend at a gospel singing convention, he and his family headed home to Gulfport, Mississippi. Once home, they found their house engulfed in flames. Everything they owned was destroyed. The only thing left was a stainless steel soup ladle, used as a water dipper, that hung on the back porch.

Even from a distance, you can still see the marks of the fire. The bowl of the ladle is marked with charred black spots and pitted by the intense heat of the fire. The fire did not melt the stainless steel—its basic shape remains unchanged and usable. You can still read the manufacturer's name and the date (1927) on the handle. The outward scars it bears, however, witness to what it has been through.

It's the same way with each of us. Our past may include events or relationships that have marked us for life. The death of a parent, alcoholism, infidelity, catastrophic illness, the loss of a child, deep depression—these things affect our lives. When we turn to Jesus, we may be healed, but the marks of our past are still there.

No matter how hard we may wish those scars away, they are part of what makes us who we are. In spite of (and sometimes because of) those scars, we are still perfectly usable in God's kingdom. As Job 23:10 says, "When he has tested me, I will come forth as gold." Or even, in some cases, as a stainless steel soup ladle.

Powderful Prayers
by Mildred Blankenship, Union City, Georgia

A large family is a blessing even if sometimes it seems the work will never end and the money will never stretch far enough. My husband and I had four children, and the one thing I always had plenty of was dirty laundry! Two of my boys lived to play outdoors, enjoying every game and making sure they brought back plenty of the outside on their clothes. My youngest son, Robert, enjoyed playing, but having been born with a heart defect, he couldn't be part of all his brothers' games.

Because Robert was so ill, I couldn't work outside the home. I could only add ten dollars a week to our family income by keeping a friend's two children during the day. That little bit of money helped us buy staples like milk and bread. It also helped us pay the bus fare back and forth to the hospital with Robert, since we didn't have a car. We indulged in no frills, and at times even money for the much-needed laundry detergent was hard to find. During one of these lean times, God proved to me how very true to His word He can be.

Before I left for the grocery store that day, I realized my laundry detergent would be gone within the week. I've always loved the Lord and taken Him at His word. That's how I lived with Robert's illness and coped with the many hospital stays that were completely out of my control.

Being a woman who had learned the reality of prayer in those situations, I decided to pray about my weekly shopping. Knowing I wouldn't be able to buy cleaning supplies until the beginning of the next month, I decided I needed divine help. I simply told Jesus that I depended on Him to let the soap powder last until I could afford to buy more. I then thanked Him in advance for what He was going to do.

That Saturday afternoon, as I put the few items I could afford into my shopping cart, I fought the impulse to get the laundry detergent and leave something else off my list. After all, I needed to keep the children's clothes clean for school. But I quickly decided to stand firm and let God help me with this part of my family needs.

When Monday morning rolled around, I was busy cleaning the kitchen when I heard something outside my back door. To my delight, I found a full-sized box of a new laundry detergent hanging in a plastic bag on my door-knob! The noise had been someone delivering a product sample to my home—but not just any product, a laundry detergent! I was thrilled that God had answered my prayer so quickly. I thanked Him, put the detergent away, and continued to clean.

When I reached the front of the house, I was still bask-ing in God's provision for the small things in our life. I opened the front door to go sweep the porch, and there, to my total amazement, I found another full-sized box of the same laundry powder! By this time, I was overwhelmed by God's generosity. He had provided even more than I had hoped for. Imagine—my heavenly Father loved me enough to help me keep my children's clothes clean!

A spring filled my step as I continued my household duties. The mail had been delivered, so I ran to our mail-box to pick it up. I almost did a double take when I spied the now-familiar plastic bag hanging on the mailbox. Here was box number three of the same soap! By now I was praising the Lord and laughing at the same time. Now I had three full-sized boxes of detergent, when only several hours earlier I had barely enough to get through the day.

I gathered my latest box of detergent and headed up the stairs that led to my house and noticed something hanging on my basement door. You guessed it: another box of detergent! I had never had that many washing products at one time in all my life.

So many times we find God trustworthy in the large areas of our lives but fail to take Him at His word concerning daily events. He is the God who wants to meet all our needs. Whether it's as monumental as a hospital trip with a very sick child or as practical as having detergent delivered to the door, He truly cares. All we need do is believe Him when He says, "Ask and it will be given to you. . . ." (Matthew 7:7).

Since that day I've firmly believed that God not only does the miraculous, but He knows the value of a clean pair of jeans!

Split Screen

by Gerry Rita Di Gesu, Cape Cod, Massachusetts

Through the porch window I see my neighbors, an elderly couple, sitting in their backyard enjoying the beautiful autumn day. Relaxed in faded, weathered beach chairs, they face each other as they talk. A pink sweater covers her shoulders; the cat snoozes in the pocket of her lap. He wears a Yankee baseball cap and takes slow, deliberate puffs on his pipe. As she speaks, she leans forward, bobbing and shaking her finger emphatically to emphasize her point. Her smile and soft laughter brighten the warm afternoon.

Expressive hands punctuate his conversation as he pokes and waves his pipe in the air, punching holes in her arguments. They are in their eighties and are truly lovers. I am amazed that they have this much to discuss after fifty years of marriage. It's wonderful to see them find such joy in each other.

Between our two yards a clothesline—crowded with toddlers' bright overalls and play clothes—flies in the brisk wind. A young couple and their two children live next door, and I feel a kinship with them as I watch them raise their children and handle problems I've already faced.

The young mother opens her back door and walks over to visit her neighbors. Her three-year-old son races across the grass, clutching a lollipop. He suddenly veers to the left and charges toward the birdbath. Stopping short, he peeks at his mom and then tosses the lollipop into the water. His baby sister bounds forward unsteadily, trying to catch up with him.

Suddenly I realize I'm midway in life, between these two sets of neighbors who are sharing the lovely afternoon. My three children, almost grown, still need the nurturing and loving environment their dad and I try to provide, but they're old enough to give us more free time to reach and discover new paths to explore together. I think of Ecclesiastes 3:1: "There is a time for everything, and a season for every activity under heaven."

Peace and beauty fill this picture framed by my window. My friend and her children are a reminder of my past. I'm thankful that shared joys and tears have imbued me with an increased inner strength. In the elderly couple, I see before me the beauty and promise of what my life can be.

What a true blessing to see both sides at once and to understand my season in between.

The Thankful Chair

by Bob Perks, Shaverton, Pennsylvania

The year after a record-shattering flood struck our area, I worked for the Commission on Economic Opportunity by assessing the needs of low-income families. I was relieved when I reached the last home I'd have to visit that day. Thanksgiving Day was the next day, and I just wanted to start my holiday early. Tomorrow, like millions of other families, we would surround the table, filling ourselves to capacity.

This home hadn't actually been in the flood area—it just looked like it. The front porch steps were missing, replaced by a few cinder blocks and planks. I saw several broken windows, and part of the foundation had caved in, exposing the basement to the weather. That day the temperature was in the upper thirties with a heavy wind blowing snow from the west. The temperature inside the house was bitterly cold.

Several times young children ran through the kitchen

playing. Noticing that they were barefoot on the cold linoleum floor, I thoughtlessly told one of the youngest girls, "You should put on your socks and shoes so you don't get sick."

She asked, "Mommy, did this man bring me some shoes I can wear?"

"No, Sissy. He didn't. Go put on a pair of mine. He's right. You need something on your feet." I was embarrassed for having put her in that position.

"Well, I'm finished here. Thank you for your time. I hope you have a wonderful. . ." I didn't know what to say. How could they possibly have a wonderful anything?

I hadn't even thought about what this family was looking forward to. I just figured some organization or church would take care of them. I looked around for a charitable box of goodies but saw nothing.

"Look, I'm sorry. I know there must not be much to be thankful for these days," I said nervously.

"Well, you certainly are wrong about that! I have so much to be thankful for I wouldn't know where to begin," the mother said.

Rising to her feet, she walked into the middle of the living room. "My dear," she said, "I know this doesn't look like much, but I am truly blessed for all of this."

"See that chair? How much do you think that chair is worth in dollars?" she asked rhetorically. "Nothing. It's probably worthless even to a junk dealer. But I wouldn't trade it for anything. I sat in that chair and waited for months when my son was in the Vietnam War. It was my Worry Chair. I sat in that chair, prayed, and gave thanks when the good Lord brought him safely home to me. When they announced that John F. Kennedy was dead, I wept in that chair. When my daughter told me she was going to college because she got a full scholarship, I was sitting there and it became my Joyful Chair. It was also in that chair that I sat, slept, and cried when my father came home here to die."

Crossing the room, she pointed to a photograph on the wall. "You see this man? He's my husband, the man who has loved me for all these years. He's at work now. He doesn't make much, but he works hard for it. He paid for that chair in sweat. There isn't enough money in the whole world for the true value of love."

"Those kids out in the yard. Do you hear them? They're laughing as they play with the other neighborhood kids. How much would you pay to find something to laugh about when things aren't so good?"

Then, walking closer to me, she looked at me and asked quietly, "Should I go on?"

41

"No," I said, picking up my briefcase. "And thank you."

"Oh, one more thing," she said, sitting down in her chair. "I call this my Thankful Chair. Tomorrow when we gather round the table to share whatever meal God will provide—and He always provides—I will be thankful that He sent you here to talk to me," she said, smiling.

"I already am thankful," I replied. On my way home, I reflected on all she had said. I realized that family didn't need me or anyone else. They had their faith and grateful hearts. On the contrary, I needed them—to count my blessings, to be truly thankful.

The Matchless Gift

by Stephanie Ray Brown, Henderson, Kentucky

After my second graders finished reciting the Pledge of Allegiance, they settled back in their seats. But Duane remained standing. Duane was an exceptionally bright and lovable student. His home life, however, was far from perfect.

His mother was a single parent who had a drinking problem and an abusive boyfriend. Duane and his three younger sisters were often taken out of the home until Social Services thought it was safe for them to return. One reason I feared for his safety was because Duane was often burned with cigarettes as he tried to protect his sisters.

Thinking that maybe he had faced a bad night, I walked over to him to see what was the matter. He looked at me with dark brown eyes filled with hurt and disappointment.

"Mrs. Brown, aren't you going to open my Christmas present?" he asked. "I put it on your desk."

As I looked at my desk, I only saw an avalanche of

papers, stickers, and books. Seeing my puzzled look, Duane went to the front of the room and retrieved his gift from my desk. As he handed it to me, I noticed the wrapping paper was a napkin from the lunchroom.

I carefully removed the napkin to see a matchbox. Although I'd been a teacher for only three months, I'd learned the important lesson of asking a child to explain a picture or, in this case, a gift, instead of disappointing him with a wrong guess. So I asked Duane to tell me about his gift.

First, Duane told me that I had to use my imagination before opening my gift. He then said this wasn't really a matchbox but a jewelry box. Inside, if I would use my imagination, I would find two precious gems.

As I opened my jewelry box, I was surprised to see—and smell—two beer caps. Duane said that instead of beer caps, they were really two precious silver earrings. He had noticed that I never wore earrings and wanted me to have some pretty ones.

I was touched by the thoughtfulness of this child's precious gift. One of my ears was slightly deformed. Fearing that wearing earrings might draw attention to the ear, I never wore them. But how could I not wear these precious earrings given by this special child? As I placed the earrings on my ears with masking tape, my class clapped, and Duane stood proudly beside me.

Every year after that, the matchbox remained on my desk. It reminded me of this child's kindness and the wonderful lessons he taught me.

Although his situation at home was not the best, Duane continued to see the good in life. The beer caps were an ugly reminder of some problems at home, but Duane had made them into something beautiful—two precious gems. Although my ear was deformed, Duane still wanted me to have pretty earrings. Even though the matchbox once held the matches used to light the cigarettes that had painfully burned his skin, his surprisingly tender heart allowed us all to see it as a treasure box instead of a dangerous weapon.

Although Duane did not have money, he still wanted to give. Much like the widow and her two mites, Duane gave all he had—his heart.

Whenever I see Duane's gift on my desk, it encourages me. If I have trouble reaching a student, I try to be like Duane and give that student a piece of my heart. When I face a trying day, one glance at the matchbox reminds me of the small boy who had a tough day every day—and night—but still could find the treasures among the trash.

Out of the good heart of a second-grade boy, one teacher will always have a gift to treasure. Many holiday seasons have come and gone, but the memory of my matchbox gift will never fail to warm my heart.

Press On!

by Linda LaMar Jewell, Albuquerque, New Mexico

Tired and grumpy, I thumped the iron down and closed my eyes. "Oh, Lord, this is boring. My feet hurt. My back hurts. I'm tired of ironing."

When I opened my eyes, the blank wall stared back at me. Sighing, I returned my focus to the collar of a white cotton blouse that soon reflected my rumpled attitude. In my rush to finish my least favorite Saturday afternoon chore, I had pressed in some creases while pressing out others.

A few blouses later, I glanced over my shoulder. The summer afternoon beckoned me. I set down the iron, wandered to the open patio door, and rested my eyes on the patch of green lawn beneath lazy clouds drifting through blue sky.

"God," I exclaimed, "Your creation is more interesting than a blank wall!"

Excited, I raced back to the ironing board and

47

flipped it around so I could face the open patio door instead of the wall.

I now iron in my usual spot, but I've turned my feet and my outlook 180 degrees. Without this change of viewpoint, I would have missed the small delights of watching a butterfly cotillion and seeing robins pirating cherries.

These days I don't always recall what I've just ironed, but I do remember the changing seasons. Orange and yellow cosmos dance outside the patio door in response to summer's sunlight kisses. Autumn's setting sun is a stained-glass glow through the maroon ornamental crabapple tree. Quiet winter's snow outlines the garden path, and springtime cheers the progress of a blossom parade.

Intrigued by the bounty of God's beauty, I feel more refreshed after ironing since I've changed my perspective. I look forward to this respite, watching the ever-changing seasons. Ironing at a more leisurely pace, I also fabricate fewer new wrinkles.

While my hands are on automatic pilot, my eyes are resting on the scene the Master Gardener creates outside my patio door. I watch God paint my personal, wall-sized Monet—a forever-changing exhibit of His glory.

When we're fretting about our least favorite chores, maybe we just need to change our point of view. We should remember Philippians 4:8, "Whatever is lovely. . .if anything is excellent or praiseworthy—think about such things." God always has a blessing waiting for us. We may just need to turn the ironing board around to see it.

Sweet Surrender

by Delores Christian Liesner, Racine, Wisconsin

As the door swung open, I was shocked. I hardly recognized Patti. Her face and bald head were swollen from medication. The only hair the brain surgery and chemotherapy had left was a limp rooster-comb patch drooping above her forehead.

Had it been only a few weeks since she had experienced those alarming memory lapses? A coworker had suggested she have it checked out, and all of us who knew her held our breath when she called only hours later with the diagnosis of malignant brain tumors.

Surgery quickly followed. When Patti called work with an update of her condition, she sent a message with a coworker to tell me that her vision was impaired. She hoped I would know where to get her a large-print Bible. A silent wonder filled me as I thought about the large-print Bible my friend Irene had teasingly offered me the month before. "You never know when you'll need this."

Shortly after that I received another message to call Patti. When I called her, she asked, "Would you come to see me?"

Honored, yet afraid, I prayed frantically during the drive to her home. How could I help someone through a valley I'd never been through and didn't even like to think about? I remembered the peace I'd known as God's Word had replaced fears and doubts so many times in the past. Surrendering myself to be God's instrument, I walked to Patti's door and stood before her.

Her blue eyes gleamed in recognition. Her familiar voice echoed from within a distorted body. She struggled to hand me the huge maroon, large-print Bible and simply said, "Show me."

Only three verses came to mind as I silently prayed for the wisdom to meet her need. As she slowly read from John 5:24 and touched the two words "not be condemned," she gasped with delight and tossed me a radiant smile. I was about to go on to the next verse when she grabbed my wrist and cried, "Wait! Get a highlighter!"

I went to the table she indicated and returned to her with a yellow marker, watching her carefully mark the words for later reference. "Okay," she said eagerly, "I'm ready now for the next one." Her voice raised in excitement with each word of 1 John 5:11–13, "I write these things. . . that you may know that you have eternal life."

She held the edge of her chair excitedly. "I can know, I can know," she chanted. "I don't have to wonder or hope anymore. I can know."

Again, she reminded me of her short-term memory loss, and she read the verses again as she marked them. This time she put her name in place of the word "you." Her face glowed with joy.

Finally, we looked in the first chapter of Ephesians, which talks about those of us who are in Christ. Our tears mingled as we talked about the goals she wanted to reach before she died. We discussed ways she could accomplish them. Her joy seemed limitless and gave wings to my feet as I headed home, humbled and awed by the experience. Her excited response to concepts I had known for years replayed in my mind and lifted my heart.

Patti and I had several more wonderful visits before she died. She laughed. Although she often did not remember what she had eaten for dinner or who had visited her that day, she remembered those verses. It's more important, she assured me, to remember the big things: God, her family, and her friends loved her. She so looked forward to seeing Jesus.

Sometimes I wonder what made her call me. It humbles me to know that others are watching and listening even when we are not aware. Though she asked me to come give her comfort, I realized that in her joy I had also been given a gift. That was the day I lost the fear of death.

Putting Away the Pity Party
by Debbie Hannah Skinner, Amarillo, Texas

I was so disappointed with God. Two years after my husband was caught in a "corporate downsizing," our family moved to the Dallas area for his new job. It seemed that everything in my life had changed for the worse. My job as a teacher, once a joy, was now a drudgery. Our finances were tighter than they had ever been in our twelve-year marriage. My dream to work from home was dashed. To make matters worse, I saw no hope for change on the horizon.

As I grew increasingly bitter and angry about my circumstances, I drew on my training as a home economics teacher and started throwing a party. This was not your typical social event; it was a pity party.

As I look back at those dark days, it was as though I was carrying around my own invisible Portable Pity Party Pack. It did not contain traditional party supplies of plates, napkins, and cups. It did, however, come with a script that helped me turn every conversation toward my unfortunate circumstances. It led me to overuse words like "if only" and "things were so much better when. . ."

The Portable Pity Party Pack needed a warning label: "Use at your own risk. Some people will avoid you when you approach them carrying this pack." Nevertheless, I never left home without it. I took it to church. I carried it into my classroom. It was my constant companion.

At the peak of my pity party, we received a phone call from my in-laws telling us that Nanna and Granddad, my husband's grandparents in Missouri, needed some encouragement. Granddad's health was quickly deteriorating, and Nanna's blood pressure was skyrocketing as she went to care for him every day in the nursing home. We had a three-day weekend approaching, so we called Nanna to tell her we were coming to visit. She welcomed us.

That weekend my husband and daughter went to the nursing home to be with Granddad while Nanna and I stayed at her house. We had a nice visit that day, but as always, I had my Portable Pity Party Pack with me. Nanna sat in her recliner and did not make any comments about my steady stream of complaints. Instead, she listened quietly as I discharged my discontent and disillusionment with God.

The morning we were leaving to return home, Nanna treated us to breakfast before we hit the road. She took us to the best spot in town, the local truck stop. As we went in the door, she carefully slipped a piece of paper in my hand. When we sat down, I discreetly looked at it. On one side, the name of some drug company was printed. (Granddad had been the doctor in their small town and had accumulated countless pens and notepads from pharmaceutical companies.)

At first I thought Nanna was trying to tell me I needed an antidepressant, but when I unfolded the paper, I immediately saw the note. Nanna had written, "Be joyful always; pray continually; give thanks in all circumstances, for this is God's will for you in Christ Jesus." It was straight out of 1 Thessalonians 5:16–18.

Nanna was not the doctor in her family, but she gave me a prescription for the bitterness that ailed me. She had listened to me spew my sorrows while saying nothing about her sad circumstances of watching the health of the man she'd loved for more than fifty years deteriorate before her eyes. She knew what it meant to suffer loss. But from her years of reading the Bible, she also knew exactly what I needed to make it through my current circumstances. She could see through my pity party and gave me the powerful pieces of God's Word that sustained her and to which I needed to cling.

As we made our way back toward home, those precious words, "For this is God's will for you in Christ Jesus," resounded in my heart. I had been so busy fighting my circumstances that I stopped being thankful to God for the countless blessings He had given me. It was as though He whispered through those verses, "Debbie, it's time to put away the pity party."

In the time since Nanna slipped me that note, God eventually allowed some of my external circumstances to change. But a deeper, internal adjustment in my heart came first.

A Mustard Seed of Faith
by Bea Sheftel, Manchester, Connecticut

We were in a small building in Willimantic, Connecticut. Our friend had asked us to come visit her fellowship. It was called the Burning Bush Truth for Youth Ministry. The first thing I noticed was a poster on the wall with a man and woman. They had heart-shaped holes in their chests. The logo said, "God will fill the empty place in your heart."

Most of the others in the room were young like us. We sat on the floor to pray. Despite the lack of furniture, joy filled that room. I listened carefully as the minister spoke about God's love. A couple of people, including several former drug addicts, told what God had done in their lives. I felt restless. I had been raised a Christian but lately had strayed from the path. We no longer went to church and rarely prayed.

The minister ended the service asking if anyone wished to have Jesus come into his or her heart. I lifted my hand. He prayed for those of us who raised our hands. The more he prayed, the more I felt as if a heavy burden had been lifted from my shoulders. I felt as if I could soar like a kite on a windy day. My husband and young son soon joined me in dedicating our lives to our Lord.

At first God's grace was sufficient. We had a period of respite in His arms as we went about our ordinary days with silly grins on our faces and happiness in our hearts. Problems, however, were on the horizon. My husband was out of work. We had no idea what we'd do when his unemployment benefits ended in two weeks. I claimed the Bible's promise—if we gave to the Lord, He'd give back to us. So we sold our TV to make a donation to our fellowship.

After my husband spent a day looking for work, he came home discouraged. I poured him a cup of tea and asked if he wanted to pray. At the kitchen table we held hands and prayed out loud. I said, "Lord, I have that mustard seed of faith You said could move mountains. Please move this mountain. Let my husband get a job so we can pay our bills."

After praying, I had the sudden urge to write down the kinds of jobs my husband liked. Pulling out a notebook, I asked, "What type of work do you like?"

"I like to work outside," he said. I wrote that down.

"What else?"

"I like to paint and work on lawns. I like driving and working with other men." My husband continued. We couldn't think of any job that incorporated all of those things, but we prayed and looked to God for an answer.

Our other immediate problem was groceries. After paying our rent and utilities, we had practically nothing left for food. Again I said, "Let's make a list and pray for the food we need."

My three-year-old son started the list off with peanut butter and jelly and a candy bar.

"Oh, Rob," I said, "a candy bar would be a nice treat, but the peanut butter and jelly is a good idea."

My husband said, "Write it down anyway. And put down a steak for me."

I laughed, thinking of practicalities, and said, "How about hamburger? I can stretch that for a number of meals."

He shrugged nonchalantly. "Okay, hamburger. Write down the steak anyway, and add a big bag of potatoes."

When it was my turn again, I said, "Tuna fish is my favorite sandwich. So I need tuna fish and mayonnaise."

My husband pressed me. "Anything else?"

"Well. I'd love an eggplant, but that's a luxury."

He rolled his eyes. "God can give you an eggplant."

"Okay, okay," I said, writing it down.

We continued our list with essentials such as bread, milk, cereal, and margarine. We added oil for cooking. I felt we should be practical, so I added pasta. A pound of pasta could last us a week.

"I like cake," my son said.

"Me, too," added my husband.

This was turning into some list! I shook my head. "Come on. God promised to provide us with our daily bread, not luxury items," I reminded them. "We don't need cake."

But when they both protested, I lifted my hands in defeat. "Okay, I'll write down whatever you tell me." So the list went on. Mozzarella, tomato sauce, salad fixings. And then we prayed.

Two days later we came home from an evening of church fellowship to find bags of groceries on our front porch. I mean, bags and bags of groceries. Of course, we realized some kind soul from our church had brought the groceries. The ministry had probably paid for it. Even so, I looked at my husband in shock. "Who could have done this? Who knew we were desperate?"

He could only shrug. "We prayed. I guess God put it on someone's heart to help us."

When we looked in the first few bags, we found tuna fish, pasta, bread, hamburger, peanut butter, and jelly—all the practical items that any family could use to get through two or more weeks. But it was the other bags that had us hugging each other and crying our thanks to the Lord.

In the other bags we found an eggplant, several jars of tomato sauce, and mozzarella cheese. There was the biggest chocolate bar I'd ever seen, which had Rob dancing around the room. There was even a steak and a bottle of Worcestershire sauce.

"Can you believe it?" My husband laughed. "I forgot to pray for the Worcestershire sauce, but that's what I like on my steak."

My heart pounded. How good the Lord was to us. Tears rolled down my cheeks as we continued to pull out canned goods and frozen foods that would last more than a month. I sat down at the table and grabbed my husband's and son's hands.

"Let's pray our thanks." God blessed us with plenty of food. Now we needed to concentrate on employment.

Every day my husband applied wherever there was an opening. He even left an application with the town hall, although they had no posted openings. They told him they would keep his application active for six months.

Only a week later, though, he got a phone call from the town hall asking him to come in for an interview. We were so hopeful. This could be the answer to our prayers for his employment. A job with the town would be steady with vacation days, holidays, and health benefits. I waited impatiently for him to return from the interview.

By the broad smile on his face, I knew our prayers had been answered. "I'm going to work at the Parks Department. I'll be working outside. I'll have a truck to drive. Sometimes I'll mow; other times I'll paint."

"It's exactly as we prayed," I whispered in awe. He nodded. We hugged and danced around the kitchen with Rob squeezing in between us.

One year later, my husband was made a permanent employee of the town. By then we had saved enough money for a small down payment on a house. All our problems weren't over, but we knew the blessings of the Lord. We learned through this experience to trust in the power of prayer. God really did love us.

Our faith has been tested many times over the years, but each time we've reminded ourselves of all our answered prayers.

We know firsthand that a mustard seed of faith can move a mountain.

The Night Before. . . :
An African Christmas Story
by Peter Adotey Addo, Greensboro, North Carolina

Christmas in my village had always been one of the most joyous of religious festivals for me. But the Christmas Eve when I was eight years old was a profoundly desperate time. My family life had been severely disrupted, and I was sure that Christmas would never be the same. I felt none of the usual joy and anticipation.

In the previous months, I had matured a great deal. In April of that year, the Army of Liberation attacked our village and took all the young boys and girls away. Families were separated, and some people were murdered. The soldiers burned everything in our village. During our forced march, we lost all sense of time and place.

Miraculously, some of us got away from the soldiers one rainy night. After several weeks in the tropical forest, we found our way back to our burned-out village. Most of us were sick, exhausted, and depressed. And most of us couldn't find our family members.

We had no idea what day it was until my sick grand-mother noticed the reddish and yellow blossom we call "Fire on the Mountain" blooming in the middle of the market-place. For generations the tree had stood there and bloomed at Christmastime. For some miraculous reason, the flower had survived the fire that had engulfed the marketplace. Grandmother told us it was almost Christmas because the flower was blooming.

Grandmother instructed us to celebrate Christmas. Those were the last words she spoke before she died that night. How could we celebrate the birth of the Prince of Peace, when, since April, we had not known any peace only war and suffering? How could we celebrate life when death surrounded us and had even claimed our beloved grandmother?

As I continued to think about our suffering, several cars approached our village. At first we thought they were cars full of men with machine guns, so we hid in the forest. To our surprise, they were just ordinary travel-ers whose detour had led them straight to us. All of them were on their way to their villages to celebrate Christmas with family and friends. They were shocked and horrified at the devastation all around us. They confirmed that the night really was Christmas Eve.

They shared their little food with us and even helped us to build a fire in the center of the marketplace to keep us warm.

In the midst of all this, my ill and pregnant sister went into labor. She had been in a state of shock and speechlessness since we had escaped from the soldiers. So as Christmas arrived, she gave birth to a beautiful baby boy. This called for a celebration. War or no war, Africans have to dance, and we celebrated until the rooster crowed at 6:00 a.m. We sang Christmas songs, with everyone singing in his or her own language. For the first time, we escaped all of the agony of the past few months.

A miracle occurred that blessed evening. Christmas really did come to our village that night. It came with the birth of my nephew in the middle of our suffering. Someone asked my sister, "What will you name the baby?" For the first time since our village was burned, she spoke. She said, "His name is Gye Nyame, which means 'Except God, I fear none.' "

Christmas came to our village that night with the birth of a baby. For us, this birth turned our village around. It personified for us the universal story of suffering turned into hope—the hope we find in the baby Jesus.

I knew we were not alone anymore, that God indeed had a purpose for us, and He would see us through what was to come. I realized there was hope, and I learned that Christmas comes in spite of all circumstances. It is always within us.

All the Pianos
by Lindy Johnson, Isanti, Minnesota

Paula wanted a piano. I had been forced to sell my sixteen-year-old daughter's piano two years earlier. Now she was hoping we could replace it. Even a used one was out of the question. My four children and I were going through hard times.

I continued thinking, however, that a piano would provide an outlet for Paula's creativity and lift her heart out of depression. It had always worked before, and I loved hearing her original music flow off the ends of her fingertips. In times past, she would come home and play something that no one had heard. It was always wonderful!

My heart swelled with the desire to give her a piano—and then sank with the reality of my financial condition. I turned to God, boldly, as I remembered the scripture, "Delight yourself in the Lord and he will give you the desires of your heart" (Psalm 37:4).

I knew I could go to my Father God with this aching

need to give my daughter a piano. I will never forget my prayer that day in 1981. I said, "Father, as Your daughter, I am asking You for a piano for my daughter. I have no money for it. Now I don't know how You will do this; I just know this is no big deal for You. You own them all. I only want one for Paula, so I am going to start looking in the newspaper for Your blessing."

Only God could come up with the rest of the story. I began looking in the newspaper for the blessing. What a feeling of adventure I experienced when I found an ad. I drove across town to look at the piano. I was prepared for whatever lesson I was to learn, but I had a history of answered prayer, so I was excited. The challenge was the money. I only had a twenty-dollar bill, and the piano was nearly nine times that amount.

As I drove to the appointment, I prayed, "Well, Father, what do You have for me?" My heart bristled with excitement—like that of a little child. I was full of expectation because I knew that this was a godly heart's desire. God would do something—but what?

The old upright piano was in good shape. I gave the twenty dollars to the woman selling it and said, "If I'm not back within a week, then just figure I'm not coming back."

She agreed to hold the piano for that long and gave me

a receipt. I walked away wondering what God would do. It was definitely up to Him. For all practical purposes, I had just lost twenty dollars (no small amount to me in those days) if God did not bring some money.

During that week, Paula's father arrived for his weekly visitation. I had not mentioned the piano. You can imagine my thankfulness when he told me he had just received an unexpected IRS tax refund and then handed me half of it. It was ten dollars over the amount I needed to pay the balance on the piano! He could have kept the whole amount, but I know God prompted him to share it with us.

Paula was out of town with her church youth group when I arranged to have the piano moved. When she came home, she first squealed with delight and then was speechless. Slowly, with her hands held up to her face, she walked over to it, as if tasting the moment. She sat down and barely touched the keys, as if touching a baby's face. Joy filled my heart to hear her play again.

That piano enabled her to move forward with her music. Two years later she performed her own song and took second place in our church's national youth talent program. Now she is serving in her own music ministry in east Texas. Recently her ministry has shown evidence of branching out into other parts of the country to serve in churches that minister to the wounded.

This miracle of the piano continues to be a blessing—not only for Paula, but also for the many to whom she is ministering. Without it she never would have come as far as she has. I am always reminded that God hears me and responds. God has a plan, and I am blessed to watch it unfold.

My Secret Sanctuary
by Charlotte Adelsperger, Overland Park, Kansas

In 1966 I drove home from another discouraging doctor's appointment. A flood of painful emotion tightened my chest. "Why can't I have a baby?" I cried out to God. "All those tests—the pain and waiting have gone on too long!"

I longed for a private place to let loose and cry. I passed St. Andrew's Episcopal Church in Kansas City. I felt drawn to go in, but practical thinking held me back. I could pray at my own church or in my own living room. Why go here?

Before I realized it, I had turned into the church parking lot. My legs felt heavy as I walked cautiously into the building. I slipped into a pew and absorbed the beauty of the sanctuary. To my relief, I was alone. Only the Lord was with me. I knelt as I focused on the cross of Christ, my Lord and Savior. He would be my Listener, my Intercessor.

Silently, I told the Lord how much I wanted to be a

mother, spilling out my fears and worries. Then I released them all into His care. A gentle peace flowed through me. I left the church with a lighter step. Somehow I knew God had heard and cared. But the uncertain journey continued. I underwent more medical tests.

Still no pregnancy. My husband Bob's face revealed sadness. Yet he remained cheerful and gave me constant loving support. A year later in July, my doctor scheduled me for surgical studies in the hospital. Just a few days before I was to go in, I was reading on our back porch when a deep sense of God's presence swept over me. Like a personalized message, memorized scripture came to me: "Trust in the Lord with all your heart and lean not on your own understanding" (Proverbs 3:5).

I was filled with incredible assurance that I would become a mother. I didn't know how I knew, but I knew it was true. Yes, I'm going to be a mother! I affirmed in my heart. I called to Bob as he was mowing the lawn.

"Hey, I've got to tell you something!"

He stopped and hurried to the porch.

"It may sound crazy, but I've just experienced the most wonderful peace from God. I believe with all my heart that God is hearing our prayers. It's like He's telling us we will be parents!"

Bob hugged me, but I knew he had doubts. Later that evening I wrote down the date, along with notes about the experience and the scripture. Prayerfully, I placed the paper in my Bible. It dawned on me that I had discovered another "sanctuary"—our screened-in back porch.

A few days later our pastor visited me in my hospital room before surgery. I told him about my experience. He responded with a prayer for Bob and me as "the couple who dares to dream." Unfortunately, the postsurgical reports gave me little hope for conceiving. That hurt. Hadn't God assured me of His promise?

Bob and I continued to pray in faith. Then a strange thing happened. In September I noticed indications that I might be pregnant. A few weeks later I went to the doctor. After an examination and pregnancy test, he said, "Charlotte, I can't believe it, but you are pregnant!" He expressed hesitation about the months ahead, but I began to cry. "God is so good!" I blurted out.

Of course, Bob and I were elated to see how God was working in our lives. We thanked Him over and over. Every day I woke up with the wonderful realization: I am going to be a mother!

Many people, including Bob, prayed for the health of our baby and me. My doctor checked me often, but it was a smooth pregnancy. I shall never forget the morning when I gave birth to a healthy baby girl, Karen Sue. I watched her delivery by mirror and burst into tears of joy. Even the doctor was excited. He told the nurses, "I'm going to carry the baby to the nursery myself."

When the doctor saw Bob, he held our daughter up. "Meet Karen Sue!" he said, beaming. When settled at home, Bob and I prayed in thanksgiving at Karen's crib each night. This began a pattern of our praying as a couple that has continued through the years—another sanctuary in God's presence.

One day when Karen was about four months old, I drove past St. Andrew's Church. I wanted to take her in, but I felt awkward. Yet before I knew it, we were out of the car. I carried her into the empty, still sanctuary. I looked into Karen's little face as I held her to me.

"This is where I talked to God," I whispered. "Here is where I prayed to be able to have a baby." My throat tightened, and I choked out more words. "You see, God in all His love, heard me. He gave us you!"

I kissed her cheek, and with blurred eyes I looked at that same gold cross on the altar. "Thank You, O Lord, thank You! I praise You!"

As I ponder these answered prayers, I know God in His

wisdom doesn't always give believers everything they want. But He does act in our lives in sovereign ways. Two years after Karen's arrival, I gave birth to our son, John. Again, Bob and I were thrilled at God's gift.

My "secret sanctuary" at a church in Kansas City holds precious memories, and God has provided more secret sanctuaries in my spiritual journey over the years. A favorite one is the "together sanctuary" Bob and I have found every time we join in prayer. God provides abundant creative places for us to seek Him and to find Him—when we seek Him with our whole hearts.

A Whirlwind Way of Life
by Nancy B. Gibbs, Cordele, Georgia

"If You'll get me home safely tonight, Lord, I'll slow down," I whispered. But at that moment, I wondered if I'd ever see my family again.

I'm not sure how the craziness all began. Many times I'd wondered how to get out of the whirlwind but didn't have a clue. The push to achieve and the vision of success filled my mind and kept me going.

"If only I made a little more money," I had decided one day after struggling with the monthly bills. At the time, I had a part-time job an hour away from home. Since my husband was a pastor, I held many responsibilities in our church. That occupied my Sundays and Wednesday nights. I then found another part-time job, which took up the four days a week that I wasn't working at the other job. Before long, I added even another job to my list of things to do.

With three jobs, one teenage child at home and two in college, the duties associated with being a pastor's wife, and a house to keep, I was exhausted. In addition, I continued to struggle to pay the bills. The extra expenses of working were enormous: the gasoline, the take-out meals, taxes, work clothes, and the "I owe it to myself money" took most of my small paychecks. However, a small amount remained to pay bills, so I continuously struggled to earn more money, thinking I would eventually be able to stop the insanity. I didn't think I could afford to give up even one job as long as college tuition and bills had to be paid.

I pushed myself to the limit. Physical ailments began to surface. How will I pay these doctor and medication bills? I wondered. But I kept pushing. I believed that one day all of this craziness would pay off. But it never did.

During this difficult period of time, my father became terminally ill. I spent a great deal of time sitting beside his bed and holding his hand. The nursing home was an hour away, so I should have limited my visits. Instead, I was on the interstate up to six times a week, including traveling for nighttime visits.

Many nights I drove home so sleepy that I felt I couldn't see straight. But I thought I had to keep on trudging along at any expense.

One night as I drove home on the interstate, an anxiety

attack got my attention. I couldn't breathe, swallow, or see well. I perspired profusely and felt as though I was going to get sick. Trucks and cars whizzed by me, making my head spin. I stopped at a rest area to catch my breath and then decided to drive the last twenty miles. The entire way home, I prayed that God would get me there safely. I made many promises to Him during that trip.

That's when I prayed, "If You'll get me home safely tonight, Lord, I'll slow down. I'll give up some of these overwhelming responsibilities, drive this distance less often, and serve You more."

I drove at a snail's pace in the right lane of the interstate the rest of the way home. I made it home safely. My husband and daughter met me at the car. When I stepped out, I became very sick. The entire next day I stayed in bed and cried a river of tears. I prayed diligently, asking God to help me escape the whirlwind.

Gradually I changed my lifestyle just as I had promised God. That night on the interstate was a U-turn in my life. God literally changed my direction. Over the next few years, I eliminated two jobs and ended up with one part-time job I dearly love. I continued to visit Dad two days a week until he left this world. My house is clean. My family is happy, and I have begun to heal. I continue to enjoy my part-time job, but I also take pleasure in full-time living. I had put my life on hold for so long that it took some adjustment to slow down and enjoy simple pleasures again. But with God's help, I became successful at that, too.

I thought jobs, money, and things would eventually make me happy. But I discovered that real success came the day I stopped depending on the world and turned my eyes toward Jesus. Placing my faith in Him made all the difference.

Doing the Dishes with Mom
by Michael F. Welmer, Houston, Texas

Before the days when we could afford a dishwasher, Mom and I would stand at the kitchen sink and "do the dishes." That is how Mom always referred to it. What we were doing to them I don't know. What it was doing to me was altering my life.

One of the first memories I have about it is that it was never a chore. Mom always made doing the dishes an act of love and service. She never complained or griped. Time after time, Mom refused the help of guests.

"The dishes will keep," she'd say.

Doing the dishes with Mom was a cleansing process, not just for the dishes, but also for me. I talked; she listened. No interference. No judgment. It was good therapy. Mom taught me the value of confession. I would disclose my feelings, frustrations, hurts, and joys with her. She would impart her love, care, compassion, concern, and counsel.

We watched the world through the window over the

sink. We eyed the traffic and the neighbors. We watched the seasons change and the weather rage. Mom consistently found a reason to direct my gaze outside the window. Mom taught me to look beyond myself to others around me and the world about me.

I hated to dry and stack the dishes. I always wanted to wash them. Mom taught me to do the things I hate. Doing the dishes with Mom taught me to take turns.

All of those lessons—service, confession, cleansing, doing what I don't like to do, and taking turns—God used to prepare me for my life as a husband, father, friend, and shepherd of His people.

Now at the Lord's right hand, Mom doesn't do the dishes, but I still do. It is my therapy. It is a way for me to summon up the precious life-forming lessons my mom taught me. It is the mechanism I use to center my life and my ministry. And it is a way for me to visit with Mom once more.

An Unexpected U-Turn
by Sandra McGarrity, Chesapeake, Virginia

Finally, we were on our way! Pulling a heavily loaded U-Haul trailer behind our Duster, we left Florida and college days behind and headed north to the new church where my husband would serve as assistant pastor and school administrator.

We had packed that trailer full and still had to leave some of our belongings behind. However, our most precious treasures, our two little daughters, were safely tucked into the backseat. They were just as eager to begin this great adventure as we were.

We left early Saturday morning, planning to arrive in time for a good night's sleep before joining the new congregation for Sunday morning services. Our only concern was our car. We had spent the last several years trying to keep the car going until Mike finished Bible college and we could afford to buy a better one. That car had given us a hard time, but it was still running.

We drove northward from Florida and were making good time through Georgia, when, just past the exit to Savannah, the car gave forth a shrieking, grinding noise and promptly rolled to a stop. Mike turned the key in the ignition several times, but the dear old car refused to summon even a spark of activity. He got out and jiggled everything under the hood, then slid back into the driver's seat with the final verdict: The car was dead.

By this time, our daughters were close to tears, so Mike said, "We are obeying the Lord, and He has promised to take care of us, so let's ask Him to help."

We all bowed our heads as he prayed, "Lord, I'm asking You to make the car start or to show us what to do next."

When we raised our heads from prayer, we met the eyes of a state trooper peering into our car. The trooper took us back to the station in Savannah. From there, we called the pastor of the church to let him know that we wouldn't arrive on time.

The state trooper's in-laws lived in Savannah, and he called them to help us out. Before long, they had graciously picked us up and driven us to their home, helped Mike get a tow truck to bring our car to their house, and then fed us a steak dinner.

We spent the evening discussing our options but

couldn't find an answer. Since it was too late to do anything else, these wonderful strangers insisted that we get some sleep and see what we could work out the next day. We gladly accepted their offer, grateful for their kindness.

The next morning our host asked that we join hands in prayer around the coffee table. He led in a simple prayer of faith that the Lord would provide. He then told us that his wife had been trying to sell her car for months. Despite quite a bit of advertising and lowering the price several times, she had found it impossible to make the sale.

He handed us a receipt for the price of the car, made out to my husband. The notation at the bottom read: "A gift of love for the Lord's work." Our prayer had been answered.

Building Dreams on Shaky Ground
by Kari West

I was carrying a pot of baked beans to a single-again bar-beque at church when I met Richard, but our year-long courtship that followed was no picnic. Shortly before Richard asked me to marry him, he learned he had a tumor behind his ear. Together, we leaned on God. While Richard underwent a risky eight-hour operation, I addressed wedding invitations in the hospital. The surgery left Richard with balance and hearing on only his right side and an unexplained ringing in his deaf ear. Besides tolerating this constant internal noise, Richard had to relearn how to walk, drive, and ride a bicycle.

We held few illusions about riding into an exquisite sunset. Four days before we were married, the Loma Prieta earthquake shook the area, measuring 7.1 on the Richter scale. It knocked down San Francisco's Embarcadero, buckled the Bay Bridge, collapsed buildings, and halted the World Series game. For two days my daughter and I lived without electricity.

Shipments into San Francisco were curtailed, including flower deliveries. When the lady creating my wedding bouquets told me this, I said, "Then we'll get a chrysanthemum plant at Safeway and whack off the flowers."

When the windows fell out of the hotel that Richard and I had booked for our wedding night and several guests called to say damages would prevent their attendance, we decided we'd settle for any available hotel room and went on with the ceremony.

Since then a lot more of my expectations have been jolted off their foundations, but I've unearthed a few truths along the way—mainly, that loss is the risk we take for living and loving in an unstable, unpredictable world. I also see how earth-shattering situations we would never choose can open possibilities and guide us to a strength greater than ourselves.

I could not have coped with life's uncertainty without Jesus. The stability of God's unchanging love provided the bedrock foundation of my hopes and dreams—my very life. When massive forces work around me, bent on collapsing my faith and buckling my sanity, God never moves. He remains stable.

From Columbine to Comfort
by Stephanie Plank, Littleton, Colorado

When my free hour rolled around at school, I headed for the library to study for a test. But then I ran into two friends who asked if I would like to have lunch at the mall instead. We left the school at 10:15 a.m., an hour before my life, and our school, Columbine, and even the town of Littleton would be turned upside down.

As we returned to school, we saw kids running across the street looking scared. I figured the school must be having a fire drill. We had a few minutes before class, so we drove around the block and headed back to the school.

A teacher stopped us in the middle of the street. "Go home!" he commanded.

"Why?" we asked.

"Just go home!" he repeated.

Jokingly I asked, "What—is someone dead?"

"We hope not," the teacher replied.

My friends and I froze. Fear filled my heart. We raced home and turned on the news. We all know how that story ends, but for me it was just the beginning.

The whole town of Littleton was seeking God, and I was, too.

I was raised to know God existed, but I didn't know what being a Christian really meant. After my parents divorced, I'd gotten teased a lot. I would walk home from elementary school, and later tenth grade, and kids would throw rocks at me. Sticks and stones may break the bones, but words kill the spirit. When my family moved to Colorado, I decided I would never again be nerdy. I decided I would do whatever it took to fit in.

I found a group to hang out with and clung to the guys in the group. I started smoking pot, and my life went downhill. The guys used me, and my heart grew cold from the pain. I started sneaking out at night, only to be brought home by the police. I watched my mother cry but continued to get deeper into the trash. I was out of control. After the shooting, my heart cried for something more. I found a Christian youth organization called Young Life. That summer kids in the group were going to a place called Frontier Ranch. I could feel something pulling me to go.

Along with my clothes, I took my anger, hurt, and bitterness. At Frontier Ranch I began to see that I was covered in sin. I thought Christ had been with me all my life, but because of my sin, I was really separated from Him. The people at the camp told me that through the blood of Jesus Christ and what He had done on the cross, I could be saved and washed clean. My heart was broken, and I fell to my knees. Jesus came into my heart. Out went the evil things that had dragged me down. My heart filled with happiness, relief, and joy. For the first time, I felt peace.

On July 24, I stepped off the bus a new person. My life began to change. My old friends invited me to the next party. With God's strength I walked away. I tried to share my faith with my old friends, but they left me.

The tragedy brought deep pain, but it also led to comfort. Through the lives of those who died, countless more were saved. I can't wait until I see the Christians who were martyred to thank them and show them they did not die in vain. So many bad things happen in the world, but God can turn pain into something beautiful.

Fruit in Every Season
by Elizabeth Griffin, Edmonds, Washington

"I'm sorry. What was I saying? I have Alzheimer's, and I sometimes forget," Mary confessed.

"That must be very difficult," I replied. Mary was the mother-in-law of my friend Kris. When Kris had asked if she could break up a ten-hour car trip across the state by spending the night at my house, I'd readily agreed. Kris was always a breath of fresh air to my spirit.

"Thank you for understanding," she said with a smile. "Are we in Portland?"

"No," I answered. "We're in Edmonds."

"Oh," she whispered.

As Kris settled her baby for the night in the other room, I learned about Mary's life as the mother of eight children and wife of an alcoholic husband.

"All my children have done extremely well," Mary said. "Some of them have done so well that they don't want anything to do with me. I think they think I want something from them, but I don't." She sat, momentarily saddened by her memories. Then, brightening, she said, "You are so kind to have us in your home."

I marveled as I listened to Mary. She had endured a lot of hardship. Now, in her older years, she was struggling with a disease that makes it impossible to control emotions, much less hide any pain or disappointment. And yet, as she told me details of her life—how her husband had left and she had worked so hard to raise her children—I saw no trace of bitterness. Mary had an air of gracious dignity that could only come from a loving heart. She had evidently enjoyed a long and deep relationship with Jesus Christ and learned the secret of having a grace-filled heart. She was one of the most thankful and joyful people I had ever met.

As I listened to Mary and enjoyed her spirit, I remembered the previous two weeks I'd spent fretting about getting older. My thirty-ninth birthday was just around the corner. Now before me sat a woman whom the psalmist described when he wrote, "The righteous will flourish like a palm tree. . . . They will still bear fruit in old age, they will stay fresh and green" (Psalm 92:12, 14).

I had expected to minister to this woman, yet she had ministered to me. She bore fruit in my life without even knowing it, simply through her heart attitude. She made me hungry for more of God. As I sat opposite Mary in my living room, I found my heart crying out, *Oh, Lord, make me like this! When I am old—and even today—give me the grace to be thankful and not bitter. Make me a fruitful garden.*

That night Mary was God's encouragement to me that He can use us for His glory at every stage of our lives.

The Birthday

by Karen L. Garrison, Steubenville, Ohio

"Hurry, Mommy, hurry! Blow out the candles!" four-year-old Abigail urged as she bobbed up and down and tugged my shirt. "And don't forget to make a prayer," she reminded, her brown eyes alight with childish wonder.

"Make a prayer?" her grandmother asked. "What's that?"

"Silly Grammy!" Abigail laughed, covering her mouth. "We say prayers instead of wishes! It's easy!"

The lights dimmed and the candles flickered. Several witty birthday cards on aging surrounded the cake. Just the month before, my older brother refused to celebrate his fortieth birthday. He did not want to be reminded that he was getting older. Now hitting thirty-five, I closed my eyes and breathed deeply. How many people, including me, did that each year—becoming less and less thankful for the miracle of their lives?

Remembering Isaiah 40:8, "The grass withers and the flowers fall, but the word of our God stands forever," I asked

94

God to help me stand firm in what He had shown me the previous year during my friend's battle for her life.

My daughter slipped her hand into my pocket—her tiny fingers finding mine as I thought about Susie. I rubbed her soft skin and sighed. Susie had been the mother of two and a wife for twenty years. Susie was young and vibrant. She had a welcoming grin, a kind heart. . .and breast cancer. Violently sick from chemotherapy, she lost her hair and began a journey of pain and endurance.

Her husband, desperate for a medical breakthrough, arranged for her to undergo experimental procedures. Nothing worked, and Susie's condition worsened. But Susie refused to give up.

I diligently lifted Susie in prayer from the onset of her cancer. Everyone who loved Susie wanted what was best for her. Some chose the "live your remaining days free of medical services" approach. Others helped her find new alternatives. Whatever their advice, Susie never wavered from one path—doing whatever she could to beat the disease. She continued medical treatment though her doctors told her there was little hope.

At night, when I cradled my newborn son, I'd think of Susie's struggle and the family who would be left behind if she died. Maybe her battle affected me so deeply because of how much I loved my own children and husband.

I started looking at life as if I were looking at it through Susie's eyes. I found a new humility and appreciation for each day. When my husband kissed me as he left for work, I'd linger in his arms a little longer. Every night I'd kneel beside my sleeping children and study their angelic faces—not wanting to take one second for granted. During that time I realized why Susie continued to fight for life with such passion.

Susie knew the secret of life. And that secret, simply, was life itself.

She wanted another opportunity to laugh and smack her husband's hand as he lovingly pinched her when she walked past. She wanted to witness her daughter's high school graduation and her son's first date. She wanted to see God's glory in another sunrise and wanted to be in the world when her first grandchild entered it. Life was not a mystery, but a miracle. And Susie knew that—right up until the moment, on a crisp winter day, she died.

"Mama," Abigail said, pointing to the candles. "Hurry! They're melting!"

My husband, holding our precious son, Simeon, gazed at me from across the table. He kissed Simeon's head and smiled at me. Butterflies fluttered in my stomach. Those whom I loved most were near.

Because of Susie's zest for life and faith in God, I stopped seeing birthdays with dread. Anxiety didn't flood me at my first wrinkles. Instead, I've embraced the joys and trials of getting older. After all, each birthday is one more year that I've experienced life's many jewels—jewels ranging from my children wrestling with my husband to a bird's morning song awakening me.

"Hurry, Mama! Hurry!" Abigail pleaded. "I'll help you blow them out!"

My son giggled, waving his hand at me. My husband winked.

"Let's do it," I told my daughter. We filled our cheeks with air and blew out the candles. The smoke traveled upward.

"Look, Mama! Look!" Abigail shouted, pointing a finger toward the ceiling. "The smoke's carrying your prayer to heaven! It's gonna be answered!"

Bending down, I cupped Abigail's beautiful face. Her eyes beamed, and I inhaled the sweet scent that was hers exclusively. "It already has been, honey," I whispered, thanking God for another year. "It's already answered."

"Honey, Will You Come Here?"
by Leone A. Browning, Fairfield, Washington

As I entered my husband's hospital room, I heard his elderly roommate moaning softly. After several moments, he pressed the call button. But it was a long time before an angry nurse stomped into the room, turned out the light, and scolded the little old man for bothering her. She never even asked what he wanted.

Before long he was calling the nurses again for pain pills, then for a drink of water, a change of position, or anything else that would relieve his discomfort. After listening to several of his encounters with the nurses, I tried to make him comfortable to try to keep him from calling for help so often.

He was grateful and quiet as I gently massaged his neck, fluffed his pillow, or dialed a phone number for him. Sometimes I just listened to him talk. I was concerned for his soul as he revealed some things about his lifestyle. I prayed for him many times.

His intense blue eyes and gratitude reminded me of the days I had spent with my father before he passed away. The roommate even called me "honey" in the same appreciative voice that Papa had.

One morning I heard him ask for a chaplain. The chaplain listened as the man said, "I don't have long to live. I need spiritual help." The chaplain prayed with him, but the little man still seemed unhappy.

The next day he said, "Honey, will you come here?"

I went to his side, surprised when he asked, "Do you know how to pray?"

"Yes, I talk to God often," I stammered. "What do you need?"

He answered weakly, "I don't think I have much time left in this old world, and I'm not sure I'm ready to die. Would you please pray for me? I need to know that God has forgiven me for all my sins."

I simply asked God to give him inner peace and the assurance that his sins were forgiven. Then I suggested that he ask Jesus Christ to forgive him and come into his heart. He moved his lips as he prayed silently. Then he looked up, smiled, and wiped a tear from his cheek.

Somehow, I didn't feel pressed to say anything else. I knew God would deal with him better than I could. I slipped away quietly, praying that his need would be met. I noticed that he was not as restless and needed less attention during the rest of the day.

"Honey, will you come here?" he called when I entered the room the next day. He reached for my hand and smiled, though his eyes were filled with tears.

"Do you know what happened to me yesterday?" he asked.

"No. Would you care to tell me?"

"I gave my life to the Lord while you prayed for me. I'm the happiest I've been in years." He beamed.

I patted his bony hand and thanked him for sharing his joy with me.

"Would you continue to pray for me? I have so many broken pieces to put back together," he confided.

I assured him that God would mend his shattered life and that I would pray for him.

Our conversation was interrupted when two ministers entered the room to visit my husband. Before they left, they stopped to talk to the little old man.

"I'm just fine," he responded happily. "I settled everything with God yesterday when the lady over there prayed with me. I'm ready to meet my Maker now."

How my heart rejoiced at hearing him speak those

words. Once more I whispered, "Thank You, Lord, for giving me this opportunity. Help me never to fail You." At times I'd grown tired of the man calling to me and had wished he'd leave me alone so I could read or crochet. But now suddenly I understood why the Lord had placed me here. . .for such a time as this.

The Long Miracle
by Debbye Butler, Indianapolis, Indiana

Jesus, do You love me? I wondered. *Am I bad?*

I knew the story of Jesus as well as any little girl could know it. I knew my prayers—even the Lord's Prayer. My big sister had taught me that. And I knew the words to "Jesus Loves Me." But I was still lost. . .to a world of seclusion, distrust, and shame.

I'd been a victim of perversion since I was a tiny six-year-old girl. My older stepbrother regularly sexually molested me. He was a teenager when he abused me, and I thought of him as an adult, so I did whatever he asked.

One day I started hiding in my bedroom closet when he came to look for me. I stuffed myself there like a piece of lost clothing. The dark closet became my safe haven—a refuge from this unspeakable ugliness that didn't go away for six long years.

My stepbrother made my world dark and scary instead of light and playful. I wanted to be a "good girl" but grew up feeling quite the opposite even after the abuse stopped. I was bad. I was ugly. I was unlovable. I believed I deserved every horrible thing that happened to me.

In that closet God filled me with His strength so I could emotionally survive this childhood travesty that haunts thousands of youngsters each year. I can't explain how I knew, even as a little girl, that God would get me through this never-ending nightmare. But there was no question in my mind—not then, and not now. I knew instinctively about God. If I had no other calm in my young life, I had spiritual peace.

I'm frightened when I think about the choices I may have made without God's abiding love and strength in my life. I only survived the trauma because He was present. Otherwise, I surely would have become addicted to drugs or alcohol, been promiscuous, or perhaps even suicidal. I did not have the power to deliver myself from the bondage of this shame.

I always have known that God did not put me through this, but that He got me through it. Romans 5:3–5 could not be more applicable: "We. . .rejoice in our sufferings, because we know that suffering produces perseverance; perseverance, character; and character, hope. And hope does not disappoint us, because God has poured out his love into our hearts by the Holy Spirit, whom he has given us."

I have always thanked Jesus for helping me persevere. But I still could not bring myself to truly forgive the man who had shattered my childhood, though I knew Jesus said in Luke 6:37, "Forgive, and you will be forgiven." So I spent several years praying for Christ to help me say—and mean—those healing words, "I forgive you."

I hadn't communicated with my stepbrother for more than thirty years, but we both regularly talked with our sister. She told me for years that as an adult her brother dedicated his life to the Lord, but my bitterness would not allow me to believe it.

Finally, one summer while my sister was visiting me, she told me, "He's entered counseling for his past sinful sexual behavior against you. And he has dedicated his life to serving Jesus."

I don't know if he had other victims; I'd always suspected it. And I don't know what made him decide to seek counseling. But knowing he had finally admitted what he had done made all the difference. That was all I needed to know—that he had confessed this sin, not to me, but to others—especially to Jesus, the Great Healer.

The next words out of my mouth surprised both me and my sister. Teary-eyed and with a cracked voice, I said,

"Tell him I forgive him."

She delivered my message weeks later, and her brother replied, "Tell her I'm sorry for the pain I caused her."

Nearly two years later my sister and I were together for another life-changing event. Our dad was dying, and the family was summoned to his bedside. It meant I would face my stepbrother for the first time in thirty-three years. He approached me in the nursing home hallway.

"Debbye, can I talk to you a minute?" he asked gently. "I want to tell you I'm sorry for what I did, and to ask you to forgive me."

"I do," I replied. "It's in the past."

At that moment we were both healed, and the burden of sin miraculously lifted from our shoulders. Once more my Lord wiped my tears, held my hand, and showed me the way to live. He took my heart of stone and gave me a new one just as He had promised.

Through the power of our Lord and Savior, I am a little girl lost. . .and found.

In the Midst of Tears
by Miriam Añeses, Ridgewood, New York

As I climbed out of bed, a tenderness in my ankle and foot reminded me of the fall I'd had a few weeks earlier. After I had my devotions and got dressed for work, I decided my journey to work would be easier on my feet if I took an express bus to work instead of the subway trip.

Sitting on the bus, I noted that the Manhattan skyline looked spectacular that day. Beautiful silvery buildings reached up to heaven against a gorgeous blue background. Traffic on the Long Island Expressway was heavy, but moving, and I arrived at my office a few minutes before 9:00 a.m.

"The World Trade towers are on fire," our reception-ist exclaimed as I got off the elevator. A group had already gathered in the conference room, where we could see the towers. We watched as flames turned to black, billowy smoke.

"How can this happen?" someone asked. "How can

anyone accidentally hit the towers? You can't miss them."

"The plane must have been in trouble and lost control," someone else theorized. I hoped it was only an accident. My worst fears were confirmed when, fifteen minutes later, a second plane slammed into Tower Two. We realized this was no accident.

As the two towers collapsed, I went from paralyzing shock to tears. Whoever was still in those buildings didn't have a chance. I covered my face and sobbed. I kept my eyes closed as if that could block out what I had seen.

Psalm 46:1–2 came to mind: "God is our refuge and strength, an ever-present help in trouble. Therefore we will not fear, though the earth give way and the mountains fall into the heart of the sea." Just then my friend Bridget grabbed my hand.

"Let's go pray," she said.

We went to my office and closed the door. I reached for my Bible and read from Psalm 46 before we prayed. I felt God's overwhelming, all-encompassing peace, as if God wrapped protective arms around me.

In the next few hours, the city shut down. People scrambled to get home. Thousands walked over many of the bridges connecting Manhattan with the rest of the city. Ferry service was available for commuters from New Jersey and Connecticut. Some of us waited it out. No one could work. Instead, we tried to reach family and friends. Telephone service was erratic, but e-mail still worked, so I let my family know I was safe.

I did not lose a loved one that morning. Whatever I felt could not compare with the grief engulfing those who had lost loved ones. The poignancy of people walking the streets with photographs of their missing friends and relatives, clinging to hope, was eye-opening.

A few days later I read Jesus' prayer for His followers (John 17). He did not ask for His disciples to be spared from problems. Instead, He asked God to keep them from evil. It struck me that Jesus may not necessarily have been referring to evil strictly from external sources. He may also have been referring to evil that pollutes our minds and spirits with fear, hatred, anger, doubt, and hopelessness. From His prayer, we learn that only the Spirit of God can protect and renew our spirits and keep us from being overwhelmed by evil.

We have a triumphant God. Evil has raised its fist at God and His people since the beginning of time, but Satan's reach is limited. Although we may feel defeated, God is our strength, and in Him we have victory.

I did not make any New Year's resolutions on January 1, 2002, but I did have a September 11 transformation. I am thankful for God's patience with me. When I spend time with Him, even when I deal with weakness, failure, anger, or depression, God reminds me that He is always in control. Nothing gets by Him—not a single tear. I thank Him for the comfort and strength only He can give.

Nazi POW #2458

by Kari West, Pleasanton, California

The thrill of combat got into my blood; but the army and air force didn't cover what the jerk of a parachute strap felt like, nor did they tell us what a German burp gun looked like. I never dreamed of how it would be to march six hundred miles, like a foot soldier, with a bayonet at my back. The sudden jerk of my harness knocked all of the training out of me, and I didn't know if I could survive it.

DONNELL F. MILLER

It was the coldest winter on record. Snow covered the dirt and blanketed the rooftops at Kriegsgefangenenlager der Luftwaffe—a German prisoner of war camp near the Baltic Sea that housed ten thousand noncommissioned officers in four compounds of ten barracks each. Inside Room 5 of Barracks 10, Stalag IV, you could see your breath. Twenty-year-old staff sergeant Donnell Miller shivered in his bed.

The coal-burning stove in the middle of the room labored to keep up with the chill—when there was fuel.

Dog tired from a fitful night of adjusting to his shifting bed—slats topped by a sagging gunnysack mattress of wood shavings—Don awaited lunch's lukewarm bowl of potato soup. Breakfast had been the usual cup of hot water, while supper was always a bowl of steamed potatoes. Occasionally, a mildewed loaf of whole grain bread and sawdust arrived.

"When we looked outside and saw the sawdust blowing off the bread, we got out the cards and started shuffling," said Don, describing how the loaf was divided among the twenty-four men. "The high card meant you got first choice; the low card meant crumbs; but nobody squawked."

The men also lived on rumors. They gleaned information from new prisoners, from ministers and priests traveling from camp to camp, and from secret radio operators inside the camp, who bribed guards for parts to manufacture a radio to retrieve BBC broadcasts out of London. "Guys were sent from barrack to barrack with the news; but in the passing, it became distorted," said Don.

For eight months, Don was a POW. Hidden among his possessions was a rumpled Gideon New Testament, a gift from his best buddy, that he normally kept in his left breast pocket. Bearing an inspection stamp on the first page, it was still intact despite the leather cover being ripped apart during a search. On his feet were rather worn shoes that he had tied to the harness of his parachute when they were shiny and new. At the time he never imagined the role these two possessions would play in the days ahead or how the values and faith that his family had passed down to him would help him survive this American moment in history.

Donnell Miller came from tough pioneer stock. His great-great-grandfather died on the Oregon Trail, and his twelve-year-old great-grandfather drove the wagon the rest of the way. During the Depression, his schoolteacher father made a living the best he could and taught Don accountability for his actions. Only fifteen years old when his father died, Don worked evenings and Saturdays to help his mother. He lived in the garage so she could take in boarders.

In January 1943 he was drafted into the air force in Oakland, California. Trained as a radio operator, he joined the 493rd Bomb Group, 861st Squadron, in Debach, England, on May 15, 1944. His job aboard a B-24 was to call the Army Airways Communication stations en route with a position report, direction, and estimated time of arrival. On D-Day, June 6, 1944, the squadron flew its first mission designed to hit strategic targets in France. They were to bomb bridges and routes the Germans counted on to defeat the Allied invasion and landings at Normandy and Omaha Beach. Above the clouds, flying in tight formation at twenty thousand feet with no visibility, Don tossed balls of tinfoil out the window to throw off German radar. Black puffs of smoke dotted the sky, and hot fragments of steel rattled the aluminum skin of the plane.

Suddenly the nose gunner screamed, "Aircraft falling at two o'clock!" Don watched a bomber from the left wing of the lead squadron collide with another aircraft. Sick to his stomach, he saw tail assemblies, wings, and engines spinning in all directions—but no parachutes. "All I could do was pray for the safety of the men, committing each man's life to the will of God," he said. "In a few seconds, twenty of our buddies were gone."

Don's personal Day of Infamy came a week later during his third mission. On June 14, after releasing bombs and being hit by 88 mm fire, the B-24 suddenly lost altitude. The right outside engine sputtered as gasoline poured over the wing. "I looked out the window and saw the White Cliffs of Dover," said Don. About fourteen thousand feet over the English Channel, the pilot ordered the crew to bail out.

"I had never parachuted, even in practice," Don said. "I just squatted and hopped off the catwalk, twisting myself toward the rear of the airplane. I waited until I dropped below the tail of the bomber, then pulled the rip cord."

The wind blew Don toward France. He landed in a two-foot-high barley field, avoiding a farmhouse roof and barbed wire fencing but striking his foot on a rock. Amazed that only his ankle was injured, he ripped off the sheepskin boots required in the plane, untied the shoes from his harness, and laced them tightly to his swollen feet. He was glad to be alive.

For three hours, Don hopped on one leg, avoiding capture, as German soldiers combed the barley fields. "Fear gripped my soul," Don said. "I asked the Lord to give me the strength to take whatever was coming. I knew things were going to get a lot tougher."

And things did. He was captured, and after weeks of solitary confinement and intense interrogation, he ended up in Stalag IV. Yet for Don, the low point of the war didn't come until the end of January 1945 after the Battle of the Bulge, as he watched thousands of prisoners—mostly

Russian and French—stagger into camp. In freezing rain, they dug through trash piles for rags to clothe themselves or wrap around their bare feet before returning to the road. Rumor had it that the Red Army was advancing from the north, seizing everything in its path, and overrunning camps. Don wondered if the thunder in the distance was gunfire.

"As I watched these poor souls and their weary guards hobble out of camp, I was scared to death," he said. But despite his apprehensions, Don knew he was not alone; the same God who had been with him in the past would be with him whatever happened. The dog-eared New Testament reminded him of that.

Late one night a guard burst into the barracks and said, "Get ready. Tomorrow morning at eight o'clock we're out of here. Take what you want. We aren't coming back." In less than twelve hours, 240 guys ripped up their long johns and created knapsacks for the journey. Escorted by armed guards and German shepherd dogs, the prisoners walked, carrying everything they owned on their backs and wearing every piece of clothing they had, including their heavy GI coats. For an hour they walked full speed over dirt roads pockmarked with ruts before weariness forced them to abandon nonessentials. Don realized his daily workouts and walking had paid off. Even though his feet were blistered and his shoulders caved in, he kept his food and the meager possessions he had brought from camp.

"We walked for three months straight—six hundred miles—in twenty-degree-below-zero weather, staying in barns at night and living on whatever food we carried from camp and an occasional potato," said Don. "A lot of guys died. I don't know how I made it through, except the Lord had something for me to do."

Don Miller weighed 180 pounds when first captured but only 115 pounds when the British liberated him on May 2, 1945, in Kittletze, Germany. Don admits that for years he hated the Nazis and blamed the POW camp commandant for violating the Geneva Convention. "Now I realize we were destroying our own supply lines by our bombing," he said. "I'm not angry anymore. And I have no worry because I'm right with Jesus."

Today seventy-nine-year-old Don Miller looks back and sees God's hand in every detail of his life—from his marriage to Julia, whom he met in 1945 and with whom he raised two children, to the construction business he owned and the Bible study he taught for twenty-five years. He speaks of the ground he covered in those worn-out shoes, that rumpled pocket New Testament that he still has, and

the verse that sustained him through the horror of war—
"For he shall give his angels charge over thee, to keep thee
in all thy ways. They shall bear thee up in their hands, lest
thou dash thy foot against a stone" (Psalm 91:11–12 KJV).
Nazi POW #2458 credits his survival to God's grace.

Joy in D-7

by Malinda Fillingim, Roanoke Rapids, North Carolina

My brother Scott has taught me more about joy than any book, sermon, or class I have ever known. Scott is the most joyful person I know. In fact, when I tend to feel depressed, lonely, left out, or in some way sad, I think about Scott and I feel better.

Scott will never write a book, preach a sermon, or be famous. In fact, Scott will never walk, talk, feed himself, or do so many other things you and I might take for granted. Maybe that is part of the reason Scott is such a person of joy: He is also a person of gratitude.

Scott was born with a severe case of cerebral palsy back in the days when there was little intervention, treatment, or understanding of this birth defect. His body is shriveled, his legs unable to move, his whole being dependent upon many medicines to keep him pain-free and alive. I grew up pushing Scott around in a wheelchair, feeding him, bathing him, and taking him to the bathroom. We had our usual

sibling arguments, but he was, and is, the most inspiring
person I know.

One summer while I was in seminary, I worked as a
summer missionary near Scott's home in Charleston, South
Carolina. Before work every morning I visited Scott in his
cottage, D-7, where he lived with seven other boys. He and
the other residents of this facility for handicapped people
would greet me with big smiles and open arms, ready to
hug and be hugged. I'd read stories and talk with them,
and we would all sing. Our favorite song was always "Jesus
Loves Me." We'd sing that song over and over and over
until I could no longer sing.

One day as we sang, I looked around me and saw several people in wheelchairs, some in casts, some bedridden,
some with oxygen tanks, some severely handicapped in
several ways. They all were singing this song with great
conviction. I began to feel sadness, wishing I could take
away their pain and suffering. Then I began to wonder
how, in light of all their problems, they could think Jesus
loved them.

On that day I asked these folks how they knew Jesus
loved them. They all began laughing at me, smiling and
clapping.

"What's so funny?" I asked. One boy named Charlie

told me, "You are funny. Of course Jesus loves me. And I know it because you told me; and you love me, so it must be true."

Scott looked at me proudly, as if I had just won the Olympics or some other grand prize. "Jesus loves me, this I know, for the Bible tells me so" is how the song really goes. But to these folks the song really means "Jesus loves me, this I know, because you show me love wherever we go." They were seeing Jesus through me. Love was their life source, and I was the conduit of God's love.

I had planned to give these people a blessing, to share some iota of joy with them, to impart some goodwill. But I was the one who walked away with blessings beyond compare. I did not hear about their pain or their inability to do so many things. I never once heard anyone gripe about what they had to eat, what they had to wear, or how little money they had. But I did hear words of glee when the ice cream truck arrived or when someone volunteered to wash their hair or take them for a walk. I heard words of gratitude when people sent them cards, held their hands, or washed their faces.

Love was about being accepting of who they were, of embracing the creation God made in each one of them. I was blessed to be in their presence, to reap some of their joy, to garnish some of their unconditional love for one another and others.

Blessings are not always the kind we see with the eyes. Some blessings can only be felt with the heart.

Jesus loves me, this I know, for the folks in Cottage D-7 showed me so.

Project Founder
About the God Allows U-Turns Project Founder

Allison Gappa Bottke lives in southern Minnesota on a twenty-five-acre hobby farm with her entrepreneur husband, Kevin. She is a relatively "new" Christian, coming to the fold in 1989 as a result of a dramatic life "U-turn." The driving force behind the God Allows U-Turns Project, she has a growing passion to share with others the healing and hope offered by the Lord Jesus Christ. Allison has a wonderful ability to inspire and encourage audiences with her down-to-earth speaking style as she relates her personal testimony of how God orchestrated a dramatic U-Turn in her life. Lovingly dubbed "The U-Turns Poster Girl," you can find out more about Allison by visiting www.godallowsuturns.com.

About the Contributors

Peter Adotey Addo of Greensboro, North Carolina, is a retired minister of the Western North Carolina Conference of the United Methodist Church. Born and raised in Ghana, West Africa, he has had a long and varied career as a poet, short-story writer, folklorist, college chaplain, and botanist.

Charlotte Adelsperger has authored three books and written for more than seventy-five publications. Charlotte is a popular speaker to church groups and makes her home in Overland Park, Kansas.

Miriam Añeses, a native New Yorker, administers an education fellowship program at a major New York City foundation.

Mildred Blankenship uses her writing talents to do God's work. She routinely writes letters of encouragement to the sick and those confined to home. Her poems and true-life stories often appear in her church bulletin.

Claudia C. Breland lives in Maple Valley, Washington, with her husband and two children. A librarian with the King County Library System near Seattle, Claudia enjoys writing inspirational essays.

Stephanie Ray Brown taught first grade for six years. Currently, she is a happy stay-at-home mother to Savannah.

Leone A. Browning has had more than three hundred articles published. She enjoys fruitful days of writing at the age of eighty-two. Leone has been married for sixty-one years to a retired minister who also writes.

Debbye Butler is an award-winning former editor/writer for a Fortune 500 company and cofounder and president of Circle City Singles, Inc. Her hobbies include scuba diving, "dirt therapy," and eating chocolate.

Sandra J. Campbell lives in Garden City, Michigan, with her husband, Michael. She is thrilled to be one of the Three Ol' Bags, a trio of travel writers who visit, photograph, and write articles about places of interest in their Great Lakes State.

Joan Clayton has written six books and more than four hundred articles. She is the religion columnist for her local newspaper. She and her husband, Emmitt, live in Portales, New Mexico. Her passion is writing. His is ranching.

Gerry Rita Di Gesu lives on Cape Cod in Massachusetts. She says, "If we look hard enough even on the darkest days, there is always a ray of hope somewhere—life is good."

Sharon Doorasamy is an American writer living in South Africa with her husband, Alan, and their son. A stay-at-home mom and freelance writer, she worked as a newspaper reporter before settling in South Africa in 1995.

Malinda Fillingim of Roanoke Rapids, North Carolina, is an ordained Baptist minister. She finds great joy in being the mother of Hope and Hannah and the wife of David.

Karen L. Garrison is an award-winning author whose stories have appeared in *Woman's World* and *Chicken Soup for the Soul*. Karen describes her family life as the closest thing to "heaven on earth."

Nancy B. Gibbs is a writer, pastor's wife, mother, and grandmother. Her stories have appeared in thirty books and dozens of magazines.

Elizabeth Griffin lives in Edmonds, Washington, and is a wife and the mother of two young boys. She enjoys writing in her spare time.

Joel Holtz lives in Vadnais Heights, Minnesota. He is a radio producer and avid reader. He and his lovely wife, Rita, hope to retire in beautiful central Oregon someday.

Shanna Hoskison of Pecan Gap, Texas, has been married to her husband, Terry, for more than twenty years. They have two daughters, Terrica and Tirzah.

Linda LaMar Jewell from Albuquerque, New Mexico, is a CLASS graduate, author, and workshop teacher.

Lindy Johnson is a published author and a member of the Minnesota Christian Writers Guild. She also writes and performs contemporary Christian music.

Delores Christian Liesner enjoys looking at life through God's love and sense of humor. She turns everyday incidents into entertaining memories and opportunities to share the abundant life God promised in John 10:10.

Sandra McGarrity lives in Chesapeake, Virginia, with her husband of more than thirty years. They have two grown daughters.

Charles S. McKinstry of Roanoke, Virginia, began writing in 1990 at the age of sixty-eight when he retired from a Cancer Rehab House he and his wife managed. Since then he has written more than fifty stories.

Bob Perks is president of Creative Motivation and a professional member of the National Speakers Association.

Stephanie Plank lives in Littleton, Colorado, and is very active in West Bowles Community Church.

Bea Sheftel has been a freelance writer and editor for decades. She lives in Connecticut with her husband of thirty-seven years, her two dogs, and her son, Rob. Her memoir Web site (www.memoirwritersonline.com) receives thousands of hits every month.

Debbie Hannah Skinner lives in Amarillo, Texas, with her husband and daughter. A public schoolteacher for fourteen years, she founded Mirror Ministries in 1997.

Michael F. Welmer received his master of divinity degree in 1973 from Concordia Theological Seminary in Springfield, Illinois, and has served in the parish ministry for more than thirty years. He is senior pastor of Epiphany Lutheran Church in Houston, Texas.

Kari West is a speaker and author of *Dare to Trust, Dare to Hope Again: Living with Losses of the Heart* and *When He Leaves*. She lives with her second husband, two dogs, and a goat named Honey. To contact Kari and/or request the free DivorceWise Newsletter, visit her Web site at www.gardenglories.com or write P.O. Box 11692, Pleasanton, CA 94568.

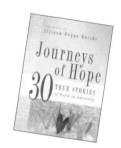

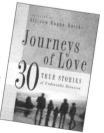